D0604344

E is for Empire

A New York State Alphabet

Written by Ann E. Burg and Illustrated by Maureen K. Brookfield

Many people helped me capture the diversity and spirit of New York. I am particularly grateful to the knowledgeable librarians and teachers, curators, and assistants who aided me in my research.

My sincerest thanks to Mary Craven for sharing with me the enthusiastic exploits of the Apple Muffin Gang. A very special thanks to my daughter, Celia, who continually demonstrates the sensitivity and creativity of a typical New York student. Thanks to Dr. Steven Burg, Professor of History at Shippensburg University, for his insight and encouragement.

My deepest gratitude to my husband Marc—my first reader and truest friend.

—*Ann*

Sleeping Bear Press
310 North Main Street, Suite 300
Chelsea, MI 48118
www.sleepingbearpress.com

Sleeping Bear Press is an imprint of The Gale Group, Inc.
a division of Thomson Learning, Inc.

Printed and bound in China.

10 9 8 7 6 5 4 3 2

Library of Congress Cataloging-in-Publication Data

Burg, Ann.
E is for empire : a New York State alphabet / written by Ann Burg ; illustrated by
Maureen Brookfield.
p. cm.
Summary: Brief rhymes for each letter of the alphabet, accompanied by longer
explanatory text, present features of the Empire State. Includes bibliographical references.
ISBN 1-58536-113-5
1. New York (State)—Juvenile literature. 2. English language—Alphabet—Juvenile
literature. [1. New York (State) 2. Alphabet.] I. Brookfield, Maureen, ill. II. Title.
F119.3.B87 2003
974.7—dc21   200215383

*In memory of Joseph and Anna, Michael and Rose, and most especially
my father, Louis, who loved New York almost as much as he loved Helen;
for Joseph who is from Brooklyn, and Michael and Rosemary
who are not; for anyone who has ever loved New York.*

ANN

*To my wonderful husband Don and our sons Ian and Colin…
for all the love and support and for always believing in me. And to Margot…
whose unfailing faith and friendship mean so much. Thank you.*

MAUREEN

New York State has a diversity of landforms, including mountains, rivers, hills, and plains. The highest mountain in our state, Mount Marcy, is 5,344 feet above sea level and is part of the Adirondack mountain range. Other New York mountain ranges are the Catskill and Shawangunk Mountains located in central New York, and the Taconic Mountains located in the eastern part of our state.

New York also boasts several *drumlins* which are smaller, oval shaped-hills formed by melted glaciers. Are there any drumlins in your neighborhood?

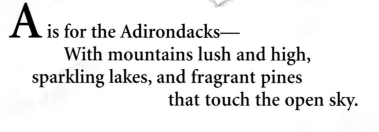

A is for the Adirondacks—
With mountains lush and high,
sparkling lakes, and fragrant pines
that touch the open sky.

Aa

B is for the Brooklyn Bridge,
opened in 1883.
The world's first steel suspension bridge
is still a thrill to see.

To truly appreciate the magnificence of the Brooklyn Bridge, it is important to remember that at the time of the bridge's completion, people were still traveling by horse and buggy. By the light of oil lanterns, hundreds of workers, many of them immigrants, labored in unhealthy, dangerous conditions to clear away tons of mud and slime so that the foundations for the bridge could be built.

Although there had been other suspension bridges, never before had the cables of a suspension bridge been made of steel. At the time of its completion in 1883, the Brooklyn Bridge was considered the eighth wonder of the world.

B b

C is for our Capital,
    once crossroads of the Northeast:
Where laws are proposed and debated,
    and state representatives meet.

On April 20, 1777, patriots met in a stone house in Kingston, our first capital, and drafted the Constitution of New York. This constitution was the set of laws that would govern New York and declare it free from the rule of Great Britain. In 1797, the capital was moved to Albany. Early New Yorkers believed that Albany was a secure location and would make the capital as accessible to western farmers as it was to downstate merchants. Albany remains New York's capital city, a vital junction for our citizens and lawmakers.

New York also served as the first capital of our nation. It was at Federal Hall in New York City that George Washington promised a new nation that he would "preserve, protect and defend the Constitution of the United States." New York might even be considered a world capital since the United Nations, a peacekeeping organization with global membership, is located in New York City.

Hundreds of years before the founders of our country drafted the constitution, Hiawatha and his friend, Deganawida, worked together to found the Iroquois Confederacy, also known as the Iroquois League. The Iroquois Confederacy brought the **Onondaga**, **Mohawk**, **Oneida**, **Cayuga**, and **Seneca** nations together as members of one group. Around 1722, the **Tuscarora** also joined the confederacy.

Some historians believe that George Washington, Ben Franklin, and other framers of our constitution recognized that the democratic principles which guided the Iroquois Confederacy could also benefit our own colonies as they struggled to unite as one nation. In 1987 Congress formally recognized the influence of the Iroquois Confederacy on our own democratic system of government.

D is for Deganawida,
the Native American chief,
who worked with Hiawatha
so there could be Great Peace.

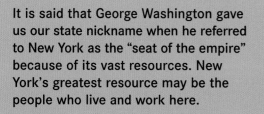

E is for the Empire State and the marvelous Erie Canal.
Opened in 1825,
this waterway carried the lumber and goods
that helped our state to thrive.

It is said that George Washington gave us our state nickname when he referred to New York as the "seat of the empire" because of its vast resources. New York's greatest resource may be the people who live and work here.

Like the Brooklyn Bridge, the Erie Canal was built by laborers who often faced dangerous conditions as they cleared away the trees and sludge to dig the Erie Canal. This magnificent waterway connected Lake Erie to the Hudson River, and brought together the outer boundaries of our new and expanding nation. The Erie Canal was a singular force in the development of New York State. Building and maintaining the canal created jobs, and new towns blossomed along the path of the canal.

Though its importance diminished once the railroad rumbled into town, the Erie Canal remains a glorious example of the vision, endurance, and creativity of people from the Empire State.

F is for the Farmer's Museum—
Watch a spinner working her loom,
learn about open-hearth cooking,
or how to make a broom.

F f

New York has a multitude of museums, each one celebrating the diverse interests and accomplishments of our state. The Farmer's Museum in Cooperstown explores our rural past while the Metropolitan Museum in New York City is brimming with art and artifacts from around the world. The Baseball Hall of Fame houses treasures from America's favorite pastime, including a 1909 Honus Wagner trading card and a warm-up jacket belonging to Jackie Robinson. The Museum of Natural History has a spectacular hall of dinosaurs and a dazzling African rain forest.

Numerous other museums throughout the state honor both our natural and cultural heritage. We even have a Cobblestone Museum and a gallery devoted to the history of Jell-O!

G is for glistening Garnet.
Grab your garden tools,
and we'll head up to Gore Mountain
for New York's State's official jewel.

The garnet is our official state gem and a visit to Gore Mountain in the Adirondacks will demonstrate why. Visitors to the Barton Mine on the northwest side of Gore Mountain can actually walk on a glistening bed of red garnet. It is a spectacular site; some of these garnets are even gem quality!

G g

THE HALF MOON

H is for Henry Hudson
and the river that bears his name.
He found a land that was fertile and vast,
though that wasn't why he came.

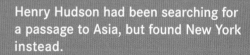

Henry Hudson had been searching for a passage to Asia, but found New York instead.

Even though New York was beautiful, Hudson wished to continue his search for Asia. Unfortunately, his tired, hungry, and mutinous crew did not. In June 1611, Hudson, his son, and five other crew members were forced onto a small boat and abandoned at sea.

No one knows for sure what happened to the hapless dinghy after it was set adrift, but according to Rip van Winkle,* when you hear a thunderstorm, Henry Hudson and his crew are playing a game of "ninepin"!

* Rip van Winkle is a character in a book by Washington Irving, a famous New York author.

I i

The United States is known as a "melting pot," a place where people of many different backgrounds come together. Many of these people were immigrants who risked everything to come to America.

The first stop for many of these immigrants was Ellis Island. Just off the coast of New York Harbor, the buildings of Ellis Island were built in 1892 as a check-in station to process the great rush of people coming to our country. Beneath the strong, watchful gaze of the Statue of Liberty, these newcomers waited in long lines to be questioned and examined. Hopefully, they would be allowed to stay in this new world of freedom and possibility.

I is for the Immigrants,
huddled on crowded boats.
They arrived in New York Harbor
frightened but full of hope.

Gelatin was prepared long before Jell-O® was introduced in 1897. It was Pearle Bixby Wait, however, who jazzed up the gelatin with color and flavor. Wait was a carpenter and cough medicine manufacturer who was always looking for ways to supplement his income. It is said that Wait first formulated this popular dessert at his kitchen table and that his wife, May, named it.

More than 100 years after it was introduced, Jell-O® is still a favorite treat. This sweetened New York blend was once served to the newly arrived immigrants at Ellis Island and to the astronauts aboard the Russian space station *Mir*!

Jj

J is for Jell-O,
   squiggly, wiggly, and sweet.
A carpenter from Le Roy
   invented this jiggly treat.

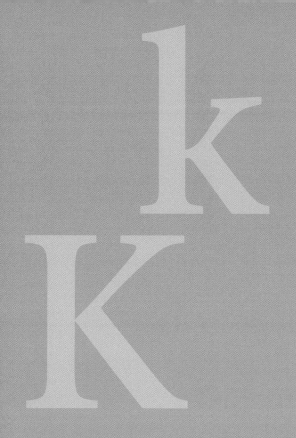

K is for Kodak.
Give a big smile aaaaa...nnnn...ddd click!
Now take it to the photo shop—
develop it quick!

Although the camera had been around since before the Civil War, it was George Eastman of Rochester who developed the photographic process we are most familiar with today. In 1888 Eastman patented the Kodak camera, which was small, lightweight, and included a developing service. Once the film had been used, the camera would be sent to a factory for the pictures to be developed and the film replaced.

The Kodak camera made it feasible for amateur photographers to enjoy picture taking without cumbersome equipment or darkroom expertise.

With her bright red wings and black spots, the ladybug is one of the most popular insects in the beetle family. Her voracious appetite for the tiny bugs that destroy plants makes the ladybug a welcome visitor in farms and gardens throughout the world.

She has been our official insect since 1989, and has even traveled into space! In 1999 four ladybugs were launched on the space shuttle *Columbia*. In a student-designed experiment, scientists sought to find out how the absence of gravity might affect the relationship between ladybugs and aphids. They named their intergalactic beetles George, Ringo, John, and Paul, after four other legendary "Beatles." The original Beatles, a popular music group from England, first landed in New York in 1964.

L is for the lovely Ladybug—
Gardeners think that she's the best.
She nibbles all the aphids
and other tiny pests.

M is for the Apple Muffin Gang.
They traveled to Albany for a cause,
and learned that hard work and dedication
changes new ideas into law.

In 1987 an enterprising fourth-grade class at Bear Road Elementary School in North Syracuse was studying how a bill becomes a law. They wanted to draft a bill that could be brought to Albany for discussion and vote. Research showed them that New York ranked second in apple production for the nation. The students decided that the apple muffin should be the official state muffin. Aided by their teacher, Mary Craven, and supported by the apple growers of New York, their parents, other teachers, and state lawmakers, the Apple Muffin Gang descended upon the capital. In 1987 then-Governor Mario Cuomo signed legislation designating the apple muffin our official muffin.

With their bushels of apples, barrels of enthusiasm, and their newly developed cream-cheese-and-walnut-apple-muffin recipe, the Apple Muffin Gang proved that children can and do make a difference.

N is for Niagara State Park,
the oldest in the USA.
Watch the waterfalls tumble and roll,
feel their thunderous spray!

Niagara Reservation State Park surrounds spectacular Niagara Falls, a natural wonder that lies on the border of New York and Canada. Although breathtaking in its beauty, Niagara Falls is more than simply a picturesque tourist destination. Harnessed power from Niagara Falls provides electricity for parts of New York and Canada. Before the discovery of electricity, local residents used the falls to power waterwheels and turbine engines.

Proximity to Canada made the Niagara Falls region active in the Underground Railroad. Runaway slaves were hidden in houses along the Niagara River. At night, courageous men, women, and children were smuggled to freedom by crossing the heavily guarded waters of the Niagara region.

n
N

As part of our state, Long Island stretches more than 100 miles into the Atlantic Ocean. At its very easternmost tip is Montauk, which boasts the oldest lighthouse in our state and the oldest cattle ranch. Completed in 1796, the Montauk Lighthouse is an expected sight. A bit more surprising may be the cattle grazing at nearby Deep Hollow Ranch. As early as 1650, the verdant pastures of Montauk were the summer grazing grounds for cattle from all over eastern Long Island.

At the western end of Long Island is Oyster Bay. There Theodore Roosevelt built his home, Sagamore Hill, at the end of Cove Neck Road. When he was president, Sagamore Hill was known as the "Summer White House." Another resident of Oyster Bay was Mary Mallon, better known as Typhoid Mary. Mary was a cook and the first known carrier of typhoid fever who did not contract the disease herself. Oyster Bay has even been linked to Captain Kidd, who is said to have buried a treasure along the North Shore.

O is for the Oldest Cattle Ranch
and the colorful heritage of Oyster Bay—
a president, a cook, and a treasure
that may still be hidden away!

Pis for the Potato Chip—
Invented in 1853
when a fussy customer complained,
"This fry's too thick for me!"

MOON LAKE
HOUSE
1853

P p

George Crum was a Native American chef at a popular restaurant in Saratoga Springs. One night, a grumbling customer sent back his side dish, complaining that the potatoes were cut too thick. Patiently, George recut the potatoes. When the customer sent them back yet again, George decided to do something dramatic. He sliced the potatoes so papery thin that they couldn't be eaten with a fork. He fried them, salted them, and sent them back to his fussy diner. Some believe that George was being playful; others claim he was truly annoyed.

Whatever George Crum's mood and reason, the diner was delighted. The Saratoga "chip" became a favorite at Moon's Lake House...and maybe at your house too!

Q is for the abandoned Quarry,
where one man working alone
sculpted a quiet masterpiece
from acres of forgotten stone.

A quarry is a place where slate or stone is cut. Some of the stone may be used just as it is; some might be crushed into gravel or sand. At one time, stone from the quarries in New York was an important export to other states.

In the 1930s, Harvey Fite, a sculptor, bought an abandoned quarry in Saugerties, New York. Harvey thought he might use the quarry to build pedestals for his art, but as he arranged and terraced the stone, he began to recognize an innate beauty. He moved his sculptures into the surrounding woods and the terraced stone became his main work. He called this bluestone garden *Opus 40* because he expected to work on it for 40 years.

Q q

Our 32nd president, Franklin Delano Roosevelt was the only president to serve more than two terms. President during the difficult years of the Depression and World War II, he consoled the nation through radio broadcasts known as fireside chats.

Having once been stricken by polio, Roosevelt was also our only president who used a wheelchair. He was, however, reluctant to be photographed in his chair. Even the FDR memorial, which opened in 1997, showed Roosevelt sitting down with a cloak draped over his legs. The cloak conceals all but two small wheels of his chair.

Finally, in 2001, another statue was unveiled that openly depicts Roosevelt sitting in a wheelchair, reminding everyone that having a disability does not impede greatness.

r

R

R is for Franklin Roosevelt,
president for 12 years.
He told us not to be afraid
of anything but fear.

Elizabeth Cady Stanton did not think it was fair that women did not have the same rights as men and devoted her life to championing this cause. In July 1848 she helped arrange a meeting in Seneca Falls to discuss the conditions of women and to formulate a plan that would serve as a blueprint for women's rights.

The convention at Seneca Falls drew many followers, both men and women. However, the 19th Amendment granting women the right to vote was not passed until 1920—over 70 years after the convention at Seneca Falls.

S is for Elizabeth Stanton
    and the convention at Seneca Falls,
proclaiming voting rights for women
        —equal rights for all!

EQUAL RIGHTS

WOMENS VOTES

VOTES FOR WOMEN

T is for Fort Ticonderoga,
where nature and history meet.
This "land between two waters"—
a place of victory and defeat.

Fort Ticonderoga, strategically located on Lake Champlain, had a short but active history. Originally a French fort called Carillion, it was captured by the British during the French and Indian War and renamed Ticonderoga, an Iroquois word meaning "land between two waters." In 1775 Ethan Allen, Benedict Arnold, and Vermont's Green Mountain Boys captured the fort from the British. This helped cut off British support from Canada and gave the patriots much-needed supplies.

Although recaptured by the British in 1777, supplies from Ticonderoga had already been dragged across New York's frozen landscape to help the patriots in Boston. Fort Ticonderoga was restored and turned into a museum in 1909.

T t

Although the most well-known picture of Uncle Sam portrays him with a scowling expression, Uncle Sam is really a benevolent symbol of our country. Few people even realize that Uncle Sam was originally based on a real person.

Sam Wilson was a meatpacker in Troy who stamped "U.S." on products shipped to the United States Army. During the War of 1812, soldiers joked that the stamped initials stood for *Uncle Sam*— and a national symbol was born!

U u

U is for Uncle Sam,
    dressed in red, white, and blue.
Beneath a star-rimmed hat he scowls,
        I Want You!

V V

M. VAN BUREN

M. FILLMORE

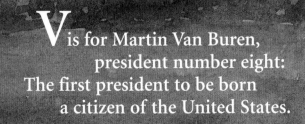

V is for Martin Van Buren,
president number eight:
The first president to be born
a citizen of the United States.

T. ROOSEVELT

Born in Kinderhook in 1782, Martin Van Buren was the first president who was born after the United States won its independence from Great Britain. Some historians believe that the slang term "OK" originated from Van Buren's nickname, Old Kinderhook.

Millard Fillmore, our 13th president, was born in a log cabin in the Finger Lakes section of New York. Fillmore was vice president under Zachary Taylor and he became president when Taylor died unexpectedly. He is credited with opening trade with Japan.

Theodore Roosevelt, our 26th president, was born in New York City. Theodore was enthusiastic and adventuresome and so loved that the Teddy Bear toy was nicknamed in his honor. He was a popular president who was interested in preserving our natural resources.

New York State has been the birthplace of four presidents, two of whom were cousins. Three are named here. Can you name the fourth?

W is for the World Trade Center:
Twin Towers that scaled the skies,
    symbol of international commerce
    and global enterprise.

The World Trade Center was built to revitalize and centralize international trade. It was a bustling multi-acre city within a city. Shopping areas and restaurants surrounded twin towers that soared into the sky, helping to define the magnificent skyline of New York City.

On September 11, 2001, terrorists charged into the landmark towers with hijacked planes. Thousands of innocent people lost their lives. For months, firefighters and rescue workers tirelessly sorted through the smoldering embers known as Ground Zero, and countless stories of friendship and bravery emerged.

Destruction of the World Trade Center had only shown that the kindness and spirit of people are always more important than the magnificent structures they build.

W
W

X

X is for eXcelsior,
the motto of our state.
It is people striving "ever upward"
that makes New York so great!

"Excelsior," meaning "ever upward," is an appropriate motto for New York State. Appearing on the bottom of our flag, beneath Lady Liberty and Lady Justice, these words remind us that we should always strive for the high ideals of freedom and justice. Why do you think that Lady Justice is always shown blindfolded? What river do you think is depicted here? To whom do you think the ships belong? Some historians believe that the sun may have been included on the state flag because the Duke of York had a badge with a sun. Others think the sun was taken from an early New York landowner's coat of arms. What else could the rising sun represent?

Other state symbols featured here are the bluebird (state bird) and the rose (state flower).

Dutch settlers who claimed the land along the Hudson River called their colony New Netherland and named their busy port city New Amsterdam after the capital city of Holland. Because of its strategic location, King Charles II of England wanted New Netherland to be an English colony. In 1664, warships were sent to New Amsterdam and the Dutch ordered to surrender. Peter Stuyvesant, the governor of New Netherland, did not want to give up, but he knew that the British forces were stronger than his own. He surrendered without a fight. New Netherland was renamed New York after the King's brother, the Duke of York; New Amsterdam became New York City.

When King Charles II died, the Duke of York became King James II. King James II was an unpopular ruler. He was dethroned and escaped to France where he died in 1701.

Y is for the Duke of York
for whom our state is named.
When he inherited the throne of England,
he became the scorned King James.

Hudson River

New Amsterdam

Duke of York

Z is for Zoot suits,
	wide jackets and baggy pants.
The hippest hepcats wore them
	whenever they dressed up to dance!

Fashion trends are always evolving. In the late 1930s and early 1940s, the zoot suit, a wide-shouldered jacket that narrowed at the waist and baggy pants that tapered at the ankles, was popular among jazz enthusiasts and musicians. One of the most famous zoot suiters was Cab Calloway, the Hi-De-Ho man. Cab Calloway was a composer and bandleader, often associated with the Harlem Renaissance. This artistic movement of the 1920s was an explosion of African-American creativity in literature, art, and music.

Although the cultural effects of the Harlem Renaissance made a lasting impact, the zoot suit did not. Some people enjoyed its extravagant style, but many others criticized the zoot suit for being outrageous. In 1942 the War Production Board began to ration the amount of wool that could be used in men's suits. The zoot suit became fashion fossil!

Z z

Empire Questions & Answers

1. What mountain range has the highest mountain in New York?
2. Why was the Brooklyn Bridge so extraordinary?
3. What was the first capital of New York State?
4. What important waterway helped develop New York?
5. Where might you find a mitt belonging to Yogi Berra?
6. What was Henry Hudson hoping to find?
7. What was the first stop for immigrants landing in the New York Harbor?
8. What state symbol is welcome in most gardens and why?
9. What is the oldest lighthouse in New York?
10. Who was the first president born as a citizen of the United States?
11. What does the motto "Excelsior" mean?
12. Why did wearing a zoot suit become unpatriotic?
13. What is New York State's official gem?
14. What does "Ticonderoga" mean?
15. Who was Sam Wilson?
16. What Native American Nations were united under the Iroquois Confederacy?
17. What did Pearle Bixby Wait introduce in 1897?
18. Why did the Apple Muffin Gang decide that the apple muffin should be our official state muffin?
19. Who invented the potato chip?
20. What was the 19th Amendment?

We've traveled New York from A to Z
and there is still so much to do and see...
We could round each letter twice again
and still not reach the very end.
Mountains, monuments, museums galore,
there is still so much for us to explore.
So much for us to celebrate
in beautiful, bountiful New York State!

Ann E. Burg

Ann Burg was born in New York and spent her happy early childhood years in Brooklyn where she wrote poetry and read lots of books. When she was eight years old, Ann and her family moved to New Jersey where she continued to read, write, and dream.

An English teacher for more than 10 years, Ann pursued her interest in writing as a hobby and had several articles published in newspapers throughout New York and New Jersey. With the loving support of her husband and their cherished daughter and son, Ann finally decided to leave teaching and pursue her writing career full time. *E is for Empire* is Ann's first book with Sleeping Bear Press. She lives with her family in Albany, New York.

Maureen K. Brookfield

Artist Maureen Brookfield lived and studied in the New York/New Jersey area for many years. She has attended the Parsons School of Design in New York, the Art Center of Northern New Jersey, and has studied with several nationally known artists. Her work has been widely exhibited and is represented in numerous private collections. Although she has worked in many mediums, watercolor has become her favorite means of artistic expression. Now residing in Marshfield, Massachusetts, Maureen is active in local and regional art associations. *E is for Empire* is her first children's book.